To

From

Date

A message from my heart to yours

My Family Recipe Journal

WITH

PRAYERS & SCRIPTURES

Aarti | DaySpring

When I miss my family, I make lentils and rice. It's the same dish that we ate once a week growing up, an essential combination passed down over generations. With just one bite, space and time disappear. I'm home, even though I'm miles, and years, away.

Family recipes are vital to me, my friend, which is why I'm overjoyed to bring you this family recipe journal!

See, I've kept one since I was 10.

I can literally see myself growing up over the pages; my handwriting transforms from bubble writing to a surely-penned cursive. Early obsessions with chocolate cake give way to tabbouleh, banoffee pie and "Mum's Tandoori Chicken."

I inherited the practice from my mother, Rosemarie, who learned it from her mother, Lucia. My grandmother filled an old day planner to the brim, each page laden with culinary secrets, traditional recipes passed down from our ancestors. My mum and her sisters made careful photocopies of their mother's handwritten instructions—each one not only a rosetta stone to the perfect fish curry, but also an earthly connection to their mum, long since passed into eternity. My mum's journal contains not only the traditional stuff, but also bears witness to her cosmopolitan palate; her Moussaka and Tiramisu recipes are legendary in our family. I know I'll cherish my mum's handwritten journal when the Lord calls her home, and I'm just as excited to pass mine on to my daughters when my time comes.

And so, here's *your* chance to capture the dishes that knit your family together over the years in a beautiful family heirloom! We designed the pages to not only capture the recipe, but perhaps more significantly, the memories attached to it. There's space to pen your additions to each recipe too. Scripture adorns the pages, and every section begins with a blessing, because to me, cooking is a spiritual practice. I pray before I cook; what a privilege it is that we get to join Him in the act of creation! Plus our creations not only sustain bodies, but pull hearts in tight, huddled close around the hearth . . . even when we don't agree with each other.

See, the Lord injected a touch of the sacred into the act of breaking bread together. It's a taste of heaven, where the barriers between we and He evaporate, where the feasting and singing never end.

My hope is that this journal reminds you of hours spent around the dinner table with your loved ones. My prayer is that you pass it onto your beloveds, so that when they follow the recipes therein, not only will a heartwarming dish ensue, but also a deep knowing that, just at that second, you're saving them a place at the grand dinner table in Eternity.

Aarti

How to Use This Recipe Journal

This recipe journal was created with your family in mind—you get to choose the sections, the headers, the recipes, and the order they go in. Maybe you want to have a section for breakfast and then another section for pastries or maybe you want to have a section for entrees and another one for pasta. It's totally up to you! There are eight color-coded sections—each with space for 10 recipes allowing you to document 80 family favorites to pass on to your loved ones.

Want to change a few of the recipes to make them your own? Go for it! After all, it's your family recipe journal. Here are some tips and tricks on adding to your family favorites to bring comfort and joy to your table.

How to Make a Recipe Your Own

The beauty of following a family recipe to a 't' is that, with just one bite, you're right back to that moment you first enjoyed it with your beloveds! But, there's also nothing wrong with adding your own fingerprint to it; heck, that's how recipes have come into being over the centuries. Here are some ideas to add a little bit of "you" to your family recipes:

1. FRESHEN IT UP

Fresh herbs and citrus are always my first pull when I'm trying to breathe new life into a recipe. Finish with a squeeze of lemon, lime, or even orange juice. Run your knife through verdant, vibrant herbs like parsley, chives, cilantro, mint, dill, basil, tarragon (go easy on this one unless you love licorice!) and either sprinkle over the top or fold them into your dish. I also like ripping herbs into rustic bite-size pieces when I want a more herb-forward sensation.

2. ADD SAUCE

Cooks all over the world recognize the value of a fresh herb sauce to liven up a plate. My Indian version whizzes up cilantro, mint, scallions, ginger, garlic, lemon and crème fraîche. In Argentina, you'll find a chimichurri accompanying your steak. In Mexico, it's called salsa. In Yemen, it's called zhoug. Whatever it's called, a quick whizz of fresh herbs, acid (citrus or vinegar), aromatics (garlic, scallions, ginger, lemongrass) and even some chiles, put a bowtie on your tuxedo of a dish!

3. PULL FROM THE BENCH

Can you sub out one of the main ingredients for something similar? Try ground pork for ground beef, kale for spinach, pears for apples, fennel for onion, smoked trout for canned tuna. You can turn a meat-centric dish into a vegetarian version using meaty vegetables like eggplant or mushrooms, and combining them with beans or legumes. There's a whole bench of overlooked ingredients just waiting for a starring role in your family recipe history!

4. ADD SOME TEXTURE

A crispy topping can change the face of any recipe:

- Breadcrumbs crisped up in olive oil, garlic, parsley
- Chopped nuts and seeds
- Potato chips, pretzels or crackers
- Crunchy pickled vegetables
- Fresh produce like arugula, radicchio, apples, radishes and fennel, sliced finely and tossed with a little dressing

5. TRY ANOTHER COOKING TECHNIQUE

- Grilling, pan-frying, deep-frying, poaching, boiling, braising, steaming, baking, roasting—there's more than one way to skin a cat, so to speak! Roast vegetables instead of boiling them to get that umami-sweet flavor and slightly crunchy texture. Charring over an open flame or grill adds a layer of smoky flavor to your dish. Similarly, try new cooking technologies: the pressure cooker, sous vide, reverse searing, smoking guns, blowtorches!

- Try it raw! After years of eating roasted Brussel sprouts, my new favorite is eat them thinly sliced and raw in a salad. That goes for beets, green beans, peas and field peas, hearty leaves like kale and beet greens.
- Quick pickles are a simple but showy chef trick: bring 1 cup water + 1 cup vinegar to a boil in a saucepan with 1 tablespoon kosher salt and 1 tablespoon granulated white sugar. Pour this over pretty much anything and you're a pickling master! Onions, cucumbers, radishes, green beans, summer squash, blanched carrots and cauliflower...not to mention fruit like green strawberries, peaches, cherries, even cranberries and raisins!

6. HOME IS WHERE THE HEART IS

Look around you. Are there people from another culture in your neighborhood, family, work or friend group? Ask them about their favorite dishes and flavor combinations. Learn how to make their favorite family recipes, and once you understand them, see how that might influence the way you cook too!

7. OPEN UP YOUR ATLAS

Pick a country that interests you and learn about their cooking culture. Why do they use particular ingredients over and over? Would those flavor combinations add another dimension to your gran's Mac and cheese? Could the flavors of Persian kebabs add a little something-something to your meatballs? The world is your oyster! Just make sure you understand the culture behind the flavors first, and it will make a whole lot more sense on your palate. Fusion is exciting. Con-fusion isn't.

8. OPEN UP YOUR SPICE CABINET

Start with just a little of a spice that takes your fancy and go from there.

- Cumin is probably the most flexible member of my spice tin; she plays well with most dishes. Coriander is a close second. Turmeric is wonderful, but go easy. She can go from warm to bitter in a 1/4 teaspoon!
- Sick of cinnamon? How about ground cloves, green cardamom, ground ginger, nutmeg, and mace instead?
- Warm spice blends like Indian garam masala, Moroccan ras el hanout or Chinese five spice powder are a great addition to wintery stews or roasted root dishes.
- If you like heat, try some red chile flakes, Aleppo pepper, coarsely ground black peppercorns, gochujang (Korean red chile paste) and Japanese togarashi!
- Pucker up! Sumac, black lime, amchoor (dried green mango) all add a sour touch that can really brighten up your dish.

If you're going to sprinkle your spices on top of your dish, toast them in a dry skillet over medium heat; that will perk up their dormant oils and bring them to life. If the spices are going to encounter heat, you can use them raw.

Contents

SECTION #1

May grace abound in all we say and do.
May everything about us
please God's heart and bless those at our table.
May our efforts be full of the sweetest fruit,
creating a safe space
for love and encouragement to grow.
May our family be strong
with patience and mercy
toward all who need it most.
And may we see the rewards of faith
in this life and in heaven.

God, help us be the family
that shows others who You are.
Help us rise above the petty and fleeting
to see others with Your eyes,
love them with Your heart,
and live with joy at all times.

(INSPIRED BY COLOSSIANS 1)

FROM THE KITCHEN OF

MEMORABLE MOMENTS

TIPS AND TRICKS

By giving Himself completely at the Cross, actually dying for you, Christ brought you over to God's side and put your lives together, whole and holy in His presence.

COLOSSIANS 1:22 THE MESSAGE

SERVES	PREP TIME	COOK TIME	OVEN TEMP

Ingredients

Directions

FROM THE KITCHEN OF

MEMORABLE MOMENTS

TIPS AND TRICKS

God has chosen you and made you His holy people. He loves you.

COLOSSIANS 3:12 ICB

SERVES	PREP TIME	COOK TIME	OVEN TEMP

Ingredients

Directions

FROM THE KITCHEN OF

MEMORABLE MOMENTS

TIPS AND TRICKS

He is the faithful God,
keeping His covenant of love to a thousand generations.

DEUTERONOMY 7:9 NIV

SERVES	PREP TIME	COOK TIME	OVEN TEMP

Ingredients

Directions

FROM THE KITCHEN OF

MEMORABLE MOMENTS

TIPS AND TRICKS

He will be with you; He will not leave you or abandon you.

DEUTERONOMY 31:8 CSB

SERVES	PREP TIME	COOK TIME	OVEN TEMP

Ingredients

Directions

FROM THE KITCHEN OF

MEMORABLE MOMENTS

TIPS AND TRICKS

He has planted eternity in the human heart.
ECCLESIASTES 3:11 NLT

SERVES	PREP TIME	COOK TIME	OVEN TEMP

Ingredients

Directions

FROM THE KITCHEN OF

MEMORABLE MOMENTS

TIPS AND TRICKS

He chose us . . . that we would be holy and blameless before Him.

EPHESIANS 1:4 NASB

SERVES	PREP TIME	COOK TIME	OVEN TEMP

Ingredients

Directions

FROM THE KITCHEN OF

MEMORABLE MOMENTS

TIPS AND TRICKS

You are saved by grace through faith . . . it is God's gift.

EPHESIANS 2:8 CSB

SERVES	PREP TIME	COOK TIME	OVEN TEMP

Ingredients

Directions

FROM THE KITCHEN OF

MEMORABLE MOMENTS

TIPS AND TRICKS

He has created us anew in Christ Jesus,
so we can do the good things He planned for us.

EPHESIANS 2:10 NLT

SERVES	PREP TIME	COOK TIME	OVEN TEMP

Ingredients

Directions

FROM THE KITCHEN OF

MEMORABLE MOMENTS

TIPS AND TRICKS

The Lord your God is with you wherever you go.

JOSHUA 1:9 CSB

SERVES	PREP TIME	COOK TIME	OVEN TEMP

Ingredients

Directions

FROM THE KITCHEN OF

MEMORABLE MOMENTS

TIPS AND TRICKS

The Lord will fight for you while you keep silent.

EXODUS 14:14 NASB

SERVES	PREP TIME	COOK TIME	OVEN TEMP

Ingredients

Directions

SECTION #2

God, bless my home and family.
Expand our influence for good
upon the lives of others.
May Your hand be with us.
Keep us from evil,
and protect us each day.

God, bless and keep my family.
Make Your face shine upon each one,
and be gracious to them;
Lift up Your countenance upon them,
and give them peace.

(INSPIRED BY I CHRONICLES 4:10, NUMBERS 6)

FROM THE KITCHEN OF

MEMORABLE MOMENTS

TIPS AND TRICKS

I will give you a new heart and put a new spirit within you.

EZEKIEL 36:26 CSB

SERVES	PREP TIME	COOK TIME	OVEN TEMP

Ingredients

Directions

FROM THE KITCHEN OF

MEMORABLE MOMENTS

TIPS AND TRICKS

We have this hope as an anchor for the soul, firm and secure.

HEBREWS 6:19 NIV

SERVES	PREP TIME	COOK TIME	OVEN TEMP

Ingredients

Directions

FROM THE KITCHEN OF

MEMORABLE MOMENTS

TIPS AND TRICKS

He Himself has said, "I will never leave you or abandon you."

HEBREWS 13:5 CSB

SERVES	PREP TIME	COOK TIME	OVEN TEMP

Ingredients

Directions

FROM THE KITCHEN OF

MEMORABLE MOMENTS

TIPS AND TRICKS

He will keep you strong to the end so that you will be free from all blame on the day when our Lord Jesus Christ returns.

I CORINTHIANS 1:8 NLT

SERVES	PREP TIME	COOK TIME	OVEN TEMP

Ingredients

Directions

FROM THE KITCHEN OF

MEMORABLE MOMENTS

TIPS AND TRICKS

A clean slate and a fresh start—
comes from God by way of Jesus Christ.
I CORINTHIANS 1:30 THE MESSAGE

SERVES	PREP TIME	COOK TIME	OVEN TEMP

Ingredients

Directions

FROM THE KITCHEN OF

MEMORABLE MOMENTS

TIPS AND TRICKS

He will not let you be tempted beyond your ability.

I CORINTHIANS 10:13 ESV

SERVES	PREP TIME	COOK TIME	OVEN TEMP

Ingredients

Directions

FROM THE KITCHEN OF

MEMORABLE MOMENTS

TIPS AND TRICKS

He . . . will forgive us our sins and purify us.

I JOHN 1:9 NIV

SERVES	PREP TIME	COOK TIME	OVEN TEMP

Ingredients

Directions

FROM THE KITCHEN OF

MEMORABLE MOMENTS

TIPS AND TRICKS

He cares about you.

1 PETER 5:7 NLT

SERVES	PREP TIME	COOK TIME	OVEN TEMP

Ingredients

Directions

FROM THE KITCHEN OF

MEMORABLE MOMENTS

TIPS AND TRICKS

The God of all grace . . . will himself restore,
confirm, strengthen, and establish you.

I PETER 5:10 ESV

SERVES	PREP TIME	COOK TIME	OVEN TEMP

Ingredients

Directions

FROM THE KITCHEN OF

MEMORABLE MOMENTS

TIPS AND TRICKS

He hears us.

I JOHN 5:14 NASB

SERVES	PREP TIME	COOK TIME	OVEN TEMP

Ingredients

Directions

SECTION #3

As a family, may we taste and see
just how good God is.
May blessings pour out
as we find our place with Him
and as we seek Him,
may we find that we lack no good thing.
May I teach my children well
to love God, love life, and live long.
To turn from things that would hurt them
and choose to do good,
seek peace, and pursue it.

God, I thank You for Your mercies
over my family today.
Our trust is in You, Lord.
Hide us under the shadow of Your wings.
Thank You that You are the one
who brings goodness to us and
does great things for us.
You are our salvation.
We praise You, and we fix our hearts upon You.

(INSPIRED BY PSALM 34, PSALM 57)

FROM THE KITCHEN OF

MEMORABLE MOMENTS

TIPS AND TRICKS

He comforts us in all our troubles so that we can comfort others.

II CORINTHIANS 1:4 NLT

SERVES	PREP TIME	COOK TIME	OVEN TEMP

Ingredients

Directions

FROM THE KITCHEN OF

MEMORABLE MOMENTS

TIPS AND TRICKS

Our inner person is being renewed day by day.

II CORINTHIANS 4:16 CSB

SERVES	PREP TIME	COOK TIME	OVEN TEMP

Ingredients

Directions

FROM THE KITCHEN OF

MEMORABLE MOMENTS

TIPS AND TRICKS

If anyone is in Christ, he is a new creation.

II CORINTHIANS 5:17 CSB

SERVES	PREP TIME	COOK TIME	OVEN TEMP

Ingredients

Directions

FROM THE KITCHEN OF

MEMORABLE MOMENTS

TIPS AND TRICKS

I will forgive their sin and will heal their land.

II CHRONICLES 7:14 NIV

SERVES	PREP TIME	COOK TIME	OVEN TEMP

Ingredients

Directions

FROM THE KITCHEN OF

MEMORABLE MOMENTS

TIPS AND TRICKS

Be strong; don't give up, for your work has a reward.

II CHRONICLES 15:7 CSB

SERVES	PREP TIME	COOK TIME	OVEN TEMP

Ingredients

Directions

FROM THE KITCHEN OF

MEMORABLE MOMENTS

TIPS AND TRICKS

His divine power has given us everything required for life.

II PETER 1:3 CSB

SERVES	PREP TIME	COOK TIME	OVEN TEMP

Ingredients

Directions

FROM THE KITCHEN OF

MEMORABLE MOMENTS

TIPS AND TRICKS

He will strengthen you and protect you.

II THESSALONIANS 3:3 NIV

SERVES	PREP TIME	COOK TIME	OVEN TEMP

Ingredients

Directions

FROM THE KITCHEN OF

MEMORABLE MOMENTS

TIPS AND TRICKS

God has not given us a spirit of fear,
but one of power, love, and sound judgment.

II TIMOTHY 1:7 CSB

SERVES	PREP TIME	COOK TIME	OVEN TEMP

Ingredients

Directions

FROM THE KITCHEN OF

MEMORABLE MOMENTS

TIPS AND TRICKS

Though your sins are scarlet, they will be as white as snow.

ISAIAH 1:18 CSB

SERVES	PREP TIME	COOK TIME	OVEN TEMP

Ingredients

Directions

FROM THE KITCHEN OF

MEMORABLE MOMENTS

TIPS AND TRICKS

A stronghold for the poor...
a refuge from storms and a shade from heat.

ISAIAH 25:4 CSB

SERVES	PREP TIME	COOK TIME	OVEN TEMP

Ingredients

Directions

SECTION #4

May our lives and our home
be a dwelling place of praise.
May our prayers reach God's ears quickly
and our needs touch His heart deeply.
May He do mighty things on our behalf.

May our praises be heard
by the people around us
by the way we live and love,
and may they echo through our children
and our children's children.
May our family name
become synonymous with hope,
joy, laughter, and delicious food.
May God be glorified
by the way we use His gifts
and by the generosity that He has given us to share.

(INSPIRED BY II SAMUEL 22)

FROM THE KITCHEN OF

MEMORABLE MOMENTS

TIPS AND TRICKS

He gives power to the weak and strength to the powerless.

ISAIAH 40:29 NLT

SERVES	PREP TIME	COOK TIME	OVEN TEMP

Ingredients

Directions

FROM THE KITCHEN OF

MEMORABLE MOMENTS

TIPS AND TRICKS

Those who wait for the Lord will gain new strength;
they will mount up with wings like eagles, they will run
and not get tired, they will walk and not become weary.

ISAIAH 40:31 NASB

SERVES	PREP TIME	COOK TIME	OVEN TEMP

Ingredients

Directions

FROM THE KITCHEN OF

MEMORABLE MOMENTS

TIPS AND TRICKS

I will strengthen you, I will help you,
I will uphold you with my righteous right hand.

ISAIAH 41:10 ESV

SERVES	PREP TIME	COOK TIME	OVEN TEMP

Ingredients

Directions

FROM THE KITCHEN OF

MEMORABLE MOMENTS

TIPS AND TRICKS

Do not fear; I will help you.

ISAIAH 41:13 NIV

SERVES	PREP TIME	COOK TIME	OVEN TEMP

Ingredients

Directions

FROM THE KITCHEN OF

MEMORABLE MOMENTS

TIPS AND TRICKS

I will be with you . . .
When you walk through the fire, you will not be scorched.

ISAIAH 43:2 CSB

SERVES	PREP TIME	COOK TIME	OVEN TEMP

Ingredients

Directions

FROM THE KITCHEN OF

MEMORABLE MOMENTS

TIPS AND TRICKS

I will be your God throughout your lifetime—
until your hair is white with age.

ISAIAH 46:4 NLT

SERVES	PREP TIME	COOK TIME	OVEN TEMP

Ingredients

Directions

FROM THE KITCHEN OF

MEMORABLE MOMENTS

TIPS AND TRICKS

I made you, and I will care for you.
I will carry you along and save you.

ISAIAH 46:4 NLT

SERVES	PREP TIME	COOK TIME	OVEN TEMP

Ingredients

Directions

FROM THE KITCHEN OF

MEMORABLE MOMENTS

TIPS AND TRICKS

By His wounds we are healed.

ISAIAH 53:5 NIV

SERVES	PREP TIME	COOK TIME	OVEN TEMP

Ingredients

Directions

FROM THE KITCHEN OF

MEMORABLE MOMENTS

TIPS AND TRICKS

My faithful love for you will remain.
My covenant of blessing will never be broken.

ISAIAH 54:10 NLT

SERVES	PREP TIME	COOK TIME	OVEN TEMP

Ingredients

Directions

FROM THE KITCHEN OF

MEMORABLE MOMENTS

TIPS AND TRICKS

No weapon turned against you will succeed.

ISAIAH 54:17 NLT

SERVES	PREP TIME	COOK TIME	OVEN TEMP

Ingredients

Directions

SECTION #5

Bless all those who enter our home.
May all that takes place here be an honor to God
and be a gift to everyone who enters.
May we receive what His heart desires for us,
and may we see all our needs met.
May our hearts find peace in times of trial,

May God be our rock and foundation.
May everything we do be built upon
His love and mercy.

May He deliver us from every enemy
that would come against us
and all He is doing in our lives.
May we always find victory in this home.

(INSPIRED FROM II SAMUEL 7, 22)

FROM THE KITCHEN OF

MEMORABLE MOMENTS

TIPS AND TRICKS

The Lord will continually guide you.

ISAIAH 58:11 NASB

SERVES	PREP TIME	COOK TIME	OVEN TEMP

Ingredients

Directions

FROM THE KITCHEN OF

MEMORABLE MOMENTS

TIPS AND TRICKS

Now if any of you lacks wisdom, he should ask God . . .
and it will be given to him.

JAMES 1:5 CSB

SERVES	PREP TIME	COOK TIME	OVEN TEMP

Ingredients

Directions

FROM THE KITCHEN OF

MEMORABLE MOMENTS

TIPS AND TRICKS

He never changes or casts a shifting shadow.

JAMES 1:17 NLT

SERVES	PREP TIME	COOK TIME	OVEN TEMP

Ingredients

Directions

FROM THE KITCHEN OF

MEMORABLE MOMENTS

TIPS AND TRICKS

Draw near to God, and He will draw near to you.

JAMES 4:8 CSB

SERVES	PREP TIME	COOK TIME	OVEN TEMP

Ingredients

Directions

FROM THE KITCHEN OF

MEMORABLE MOMENTS

TIPS AND TRICKS

Humble yourselves before the Lord, and He will lift you up.

JAMES 4:10 NIV

SERVES	PREP TIME	COOK TIME	OVEN TEMP

Ingredients

Directions

FROM THE KITCHEN OF

MEMORABLE MOMENTS

TIPS AND TRICKS

I have it all planned out—plans to take care of you,
not abandon you, plans to give you the future you hope for.

JEREMIAH 29:11 THE MESSAGE

SERVES	PREP TIME	COOK TIME	OVEN TEMP

Ingredients

Directions

FROM THE KITCHEN OF

MEMORABLE MOMENTS

TIPS AND TRICKS

I will give you back your health and heal your wounds.
JEREMIAH 30:17 NLT

SERVES	PREP TIME	COOK TIME	OVEN TEMP

Ingredients

Directions

FROM THE KITCHEN OF

MEMORABLE MOMENTS

TIPS AND TRICKS

Call to Me and I will answer.

JEREMIAH 33:3 NIV

SERVES	PREP TIME	COOK TIME	OVEN TEMP

Ingredients

Directions

FROM THE KITCHEN OF

MEMORABLE MOMENTS

TIPS AND TRICKS

Those who drink the water I give will never be thirsty again.

JOHN 4:14 NLT

SERVES	PREP TIME	COOK TIME	OVEN TEMP

Ingredients

Directions

FROM THE KITCHEN OF

MEMORABLE MOMENTS

TIPS AND TRICKS

I am the living bread . . . .
Whoever eats this bread will live forever.

JOHN 6:51 NIV

SERVES	PREP TIME	COOK TIME	OVEN TEMP

Ingredients

Directions

SECTION #6

May wisdom always be a companion in this home,
and may we always recognize the difference
between walking in wisdom
and being full of ourselves.
May we choose humility for ourselves
and grace for others.
May we hide peace in our hearts,
in our words, and the things we do.
May each member of my family
grow in strength, mature in love,
and learn the art of beautiful surrender.
May we reflect in every way
that we are a family who knows
that our bonds make us powerful
and our choice to follow God
is a choice made in strength and joy.

(INSPIRED BY II SAMUEL 22)

FROM THE KITCHEN OF

MEMORABLE MOMENTS

TIPS AND TRICKS

If you follow Me, you won't have to walk in darkness,
because you will have the light that leads to life.

JOHN 8:12 NLT

SERVES	PREP TIME	COOK TIME	OVEN TEMP

Ingredients

Directions

FROM THE KITCHEN OF

MEMORABLE MOMENTS

TIPS AND TRICKS

Anyone who believes in Me will live, even after dying.

JOHN 11:25 NLT

SERVES	PREP TIME	COOK TIME	OVEN TEMP

Ingredients

Directions

FROM THE KITCHEN OF

MEMORABLE MOMENTS

TIPS AND TRICKS

Peace I leave with you. My peace I give to you.

JOHN 14:27 CSB

SERVES	PREP TIME	COOK TIME	OVEN TEMP

Ingredients

Directions

FROM THE KITCHEN OF

MEMORABLE MOMENTS

TIPS AND TRICKS

I will send you the Helper from the Father.
He is the Spirit of truth who comes from the Father.

JOHN 15:26 ICB

SERVES	PREP TIME	COOK TIME	OVEN TEMP

Ingredients

Directions

FROM THE KITCHEN OF

MEMORABLE MOMENTS

TIPS AND TRICKS

Remain in Me, and I will remain in you.

JOHN 15:4 NLT

SERVES	PREP TIME	COOK TIME	OVEN TEMP

Ingredients

Directions

FROM THE KITCHEN OF

MEMORABLE MOMENTS

TIPS AND TRICKS

When the Spirit of truth comes, He will guide you into all truth.

JOHN 16:13 NLT

SERVES	PREP TIME	COOK TIME	OVEN TEMP

Ingredients

Directions

FROM THE KITCHEN OF

MEMORABLE MOMENTS

TIPS AND TRICKS

God, who . . . will bring you with great joy
into His glorious presence without a single fault.

JUDE 1:24 NLT

SERVES	PREP TIME	COOK TIME	OVEN TEMP

Ingredients

Directions

FROM THE KITCHEN OF

MEMORABLE MOMENTS

TIPS AND TRICKS

His mercies never end. They are new every morning.

LAMENTATIONS 3:22–23 CSB

SERVES	PREP TIME	COOK TIME	OVEN TEMP

Ingredients

Directions

FROM THE KITCHEN OF

MEMORABLE MOMENTS

TIPS AND TRICKS

The Lord is good to those who wait for Him,
to the person who seeks Him.

LAMENTATIONS 3:25 NASB

SERVES	PREP TIME	COOK TIME	OVEN TEMP

Ingredients

Directions

FROM THE KITCHEN OF

MEMORABLE MOMENTS

TIPS AND TRICKS

I will give you rain at the right time . . .
and the trees of the field will bear their fruit.

LEVITICUS 26:4 CSB

SERVES	PREP TIME	COOK TIME	OVEN TEMP

Ingredients

Directions

SECTION #7

Lord, be the peace of our hearts
and the peace of our home.
Jesus, I thank You that You are a Shepherd
who kindly and lovingly leads us.
You are working on us
from the inside out, and I pray you continue
until the work is completed.

Help us to lead others well,
always pointing to You
and being the kind of people
who bless Your heart.
Give us a legacy that has healed from past hurts,
and comforts those who need it.
May we be the very best example
for the generations to come.

(INSPIRED BY HEBREWS 13:20–21)

FROM THE KITCHEN OF

MEMORABLE MOMENTS

TIPS AND TRICKS

For nothing will be impossible with God.

LUKE 1:37 ESV

SERVES	PREP TIME	COOK TIME	OVEN TEMP

Ingredients

Directions

FROM THE KITCHEN OF

MEMORABLE MOMENTS

TIPS AND TRICKS

Give, and it will be given to you.

LUKE 6:38 NIV

SERVES	PREP TIME	COOK TIME	OVEN TEMP

Ingredients

Directions

FROM THE KITCHEN OF

MEMORABLE MOMENTS

TIPS AND TRICKS

The Son of Man came to find and restore the lost.

LUKE 19:10 THE MESSAGE

SERVES	PREP TIME	COOK TIME	OVEN TEMP

Ingredients

Directions

FROM THE KITCHEN OF

MEMORABLE MOMENTS

TIPS AND TRICKS

You're blessed when you're at the end of your rope.
With less of you there is more of God.

MATTHEW 5:3 THE MESSAGE

SERVES	PREP TIME	COOK TIME	OVEN TEMP

Ingredients

Directions

FROM THE KITCHEN OF

MEMORABLE MOMENTS

TIPS AND TRICKS

Blessed are those who mourn, for they shall be comforted.

MATTHEW 5:4 ESV

SERVES	PREP TIME	COOK TIME	OVEN TEMP

Ingredients

Directions

FROM THE KITCHEN OF

MEMORABLE MOMENTS

TIPS AND TRICKS

Your Father knows the things you need before you ask Him.

MATTHEW 6:8 ICB

SERVES	PREP TIME	COOK TIME	OVEN TEMP

Ingredients

Directions

FROM THE KITCHEN OF

MEMORABLE MOMENTS

TIPS AND TRICKS

Continue to ask, and God will give to you.
Continue to search, and you will find.
Continue to knock, and the door will open for you.

MATTHEW 7:7 ICB

SERVES	PREP TIME	COOK TIME	OVEN TEMP

Ingredients

Directions

FROM THE KITCHEN OF

MEMORABLE MOMENTS

TIPS AND TRICKS

Come to me, all who labor and are heavy laden,
and I will give you rest.

MATTHEW 11:28 ESV

SERVES	PREP TIME	COOK TIME	OVEN TEMP

Ingredients

Directions

FROM THE KITCHEN OF

MEMORABLE MOMENTS

TIPS AND TRICKS

The Lord is good, a stronghold in the day of trouble.

NAHUM 1:7 ESV

SERVES	PREP TIME	COOK TIME	OVEN TEMP

Ingredients

Directions

FROM THE KITCHEN OF

MEMORABLE MOMENTS

TIPS AND TRICKS

Do not grieve, for the joy of the Lord is your strength.

NEHEMIAH 8:10 NIV

SERVES	PREP TIME	COOK TIME	OVEN TEMP

Ingredients

Directions

SECTION #8

Let us be the family who says yes to God,
no matter what.
In the face of the unknown, yes.
When great creativity is required, yes.
When it might hurt, yes.
When it means lying down to rest, yes.
In spite of people's opinions, yes.
In spite of our own inner voice, yes.
In joy or sorrow, yes.

Let us be the family
who boldly trusts that God's way is best,
that adventure awaits,
and that saying yes to Him
is signing on the dotted line
for the very best adventure
life has to offer.

(INSPIRED BY LUKE 1:38)

FROM THE KITCHEN OF

MEMORABLE MOMENTS

TIPS AND TRICKS

Don't fret or worry. Instead of worrying, pray.

PHILIPPIANS 4:6 THE MESSAGE

SERVES	PREP TIME	COOK TIME	OVEN TEMP

Ingredients

Directions

FROM THE KITCHEN OF

MEMORABLE MOMENTS

TIPS AND TRICKS

God's peace will keep your hearts and minds in Christ Jesus.

PHILIPPIANS 4:7 ICB

SERVES	PREP TIME	COOK TIME	OVEN TEMP

Ingredients

Directions

FROM THE KITCHEN OF

MEMORABLE MOMENTS

TIPS AND TRICKS

I can do all things through Christ because He gives me strength.

PHILIPPIANS 4:13 ICB

SERVES	PREP TIME	COOK TIME	OVEN TEMP

Ingredients

Directions

FROM THE KITCHEN OF

MEMORABLE MOMENTS

TIPS AND TRICKS

God will meet all your needs.

PHILIPPIANS 4:19 NIV

SERVES	PREP TIME	COOK TIME	OVEN TEMP

Ingredients

Directions

FROM THE KITCHEN OF

MEMORABLE MOMENTS

TIPS AND TRICKS

He will make your paths straight.

PROVERBS 3:6 CSB

SERVES	PREP TIME	COOK TIME	OVEN TEMP

Ingredients

Directions

FROM THE KITCHEN OF

MEMORABLE MOMENTS

TIPS AND TRICKS

He is a shield to those who take refuge in Him.

PROVERBS 30:5 CSB

SERVES	PREP TIME	COOK TIME	OVEN TEMP

Ingredients

Directions

FROM THE KITCHEN OF

MEMORABLE MOMENTS

TIPS AND TRICKS

But You, Lord, are a shield around me, my glory,
and the One who lifts up my head.

PSALM 3:3 CSB

SERVES	PREP TIME	COOK TIME	OVEN TEMP

Ingredients

Directions

FROM THE KITCHEN OF

MEMORABLE MOMENTS

TIPS AND TRICKS

You will fill me with joy in Your presence.

PSALM 16:11 NIV

SERVES	PREP TIME	COOK TIME	OVEN TEMP

Ingredients

Directions

FROM THE KITCHEN OF

MEMORABLE MOMENTS

TIPS AND TRICKS

He lets me lie down in green pastures;
He leads me beside quiet waters.

PSALM 23:2 CSB

SERVES	PREP TIME	COOK TIME	OVEN TEMP

Ingredients

Directions

FROM THE KITCHEN OF

MEMORABLE MOMENTS

TIPS AND TRICKS

He renews my life;
He leads me along the right paths for His name's sake.

PSALM 23:3 CSB

SERVES	PREP TIME	COOK TIME	OVEN TEMP

Ingredients

Directions

Notes

Notes

VOLUME MEASUREMENT CONVERSIONS

CUPS	TABLESPOONS	TEASPOONS	MILLILITERS
		1 tsp	5 ml
1/16 cup	1 tbsp	3 tsp	15 ml
1/8 cup	2 tbsp	6 tsp	30 ml
1/4 cup	4 tbsp	12 tsp	60 ml
1/3 cup	5 1/3 tbsp	16 tsp	80 ml
1/2 cup	8 tbsp	24 tsp	120 ml
2/3 cup	10 2/3 tbsp	32 tsp	160 ml
3/4 cup	12 tbsp	36 tsp	180 ml
1 cup	16 tbsp	48 tsp	240 ml

1 QUART = 2 PINTS = 4 CUPS = 32 OZ = 950 ML

1 PINT = 2 CUPS = 16 OZ = 480 ML

1 CUP = 16 TBSP = 8 OZ = 240 ML

1/4 CUP = 4 TBSP = 12 TSP = 2 OZ = 60 ML

1 TBSP = 3 TSP = 1/2 OZ = 15 ML

COOKING TEMPERATURE CONVERSIONS

CELCIUS/CENTIGRADE
F = (C x 1.8) + 32

FAHRENHEIT
C = (F – 32) x 0.5556

About the Author

AARTI SEQUEIRA is a television personality, chef, cookbook author, news and documentary producer, third-culture kid, and chaser of the polyglot palate. She's fascinated by the fact that Jesus knew how to cook and spends way too long imagining what's going to be on the table at the heavenly feast. She's married to her college sweetheart, Brendan, and has two daughters, Eliyah and Moses.

My Family Recipe Journal: With Prayers & Scriptures

First Edition, November 2021

Published by:

DaySpring

21154 Highway 16 East
Siloam Springs, AR 72761
dayspring.com

Printed in the China
Prime: J8764
ISBN: 978-1-64870-807-7